THIS BOOK BELONGS to...

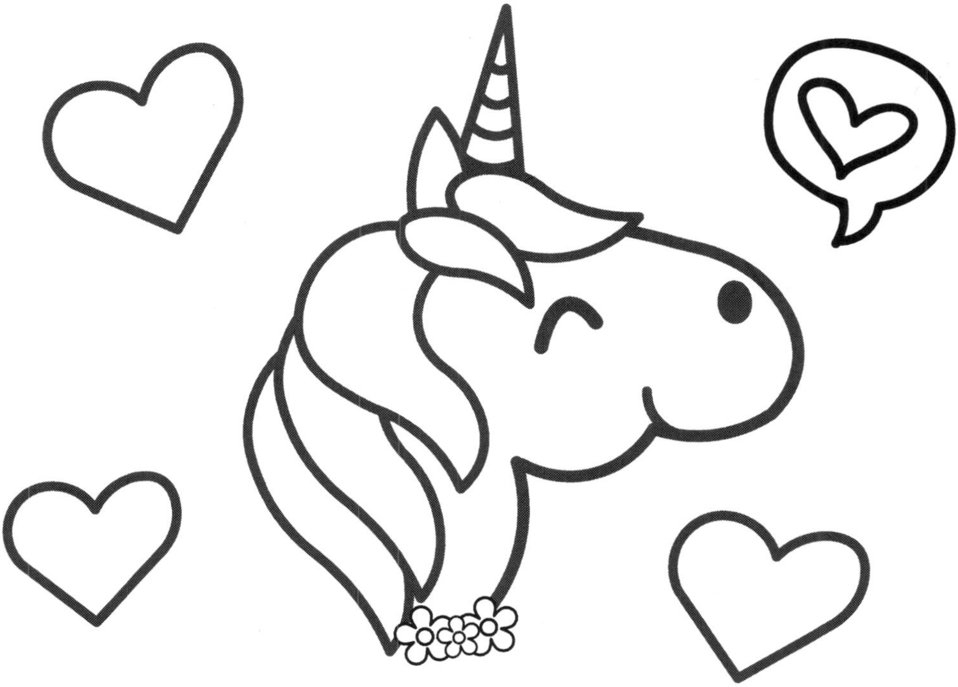

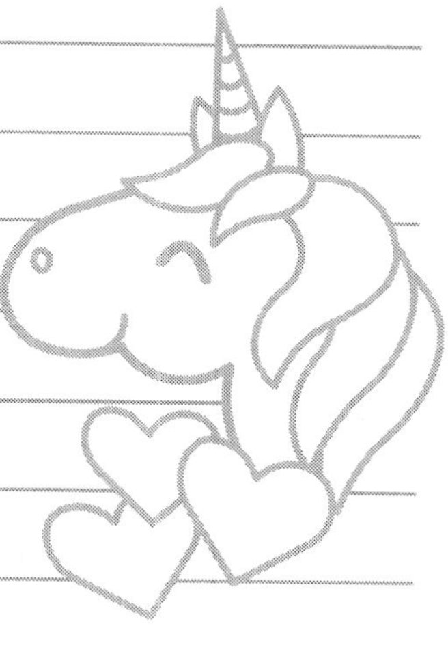

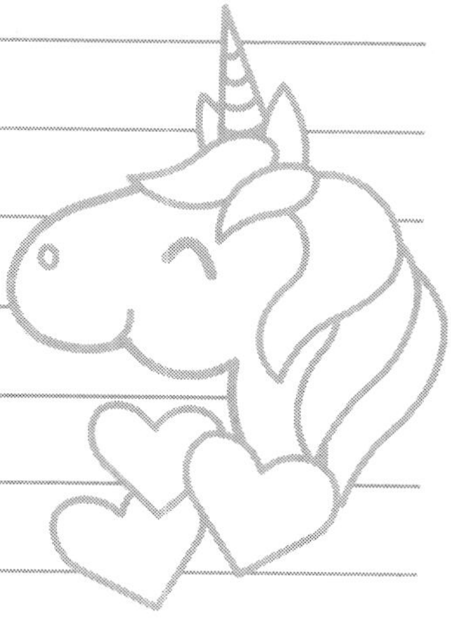

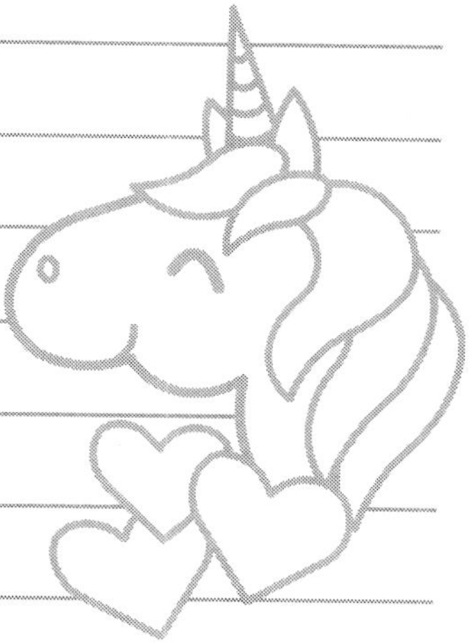

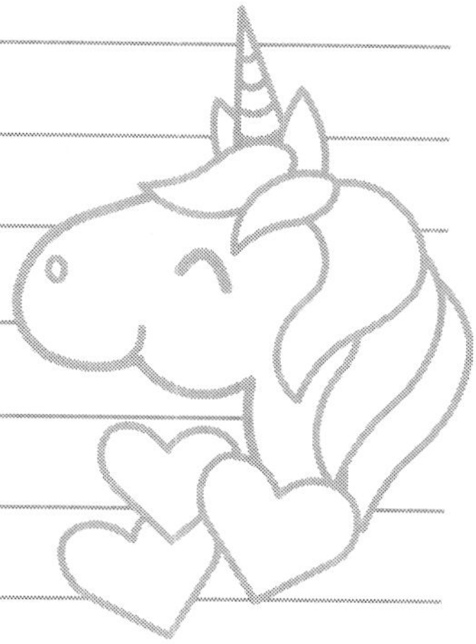

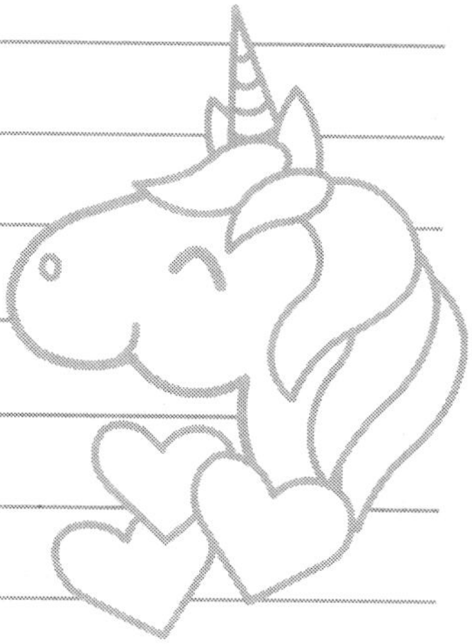

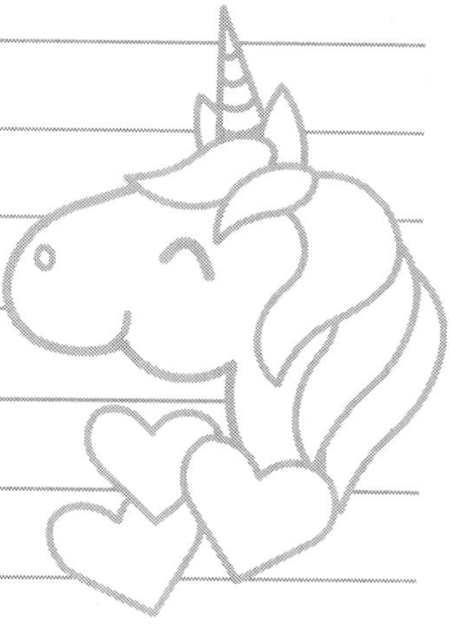

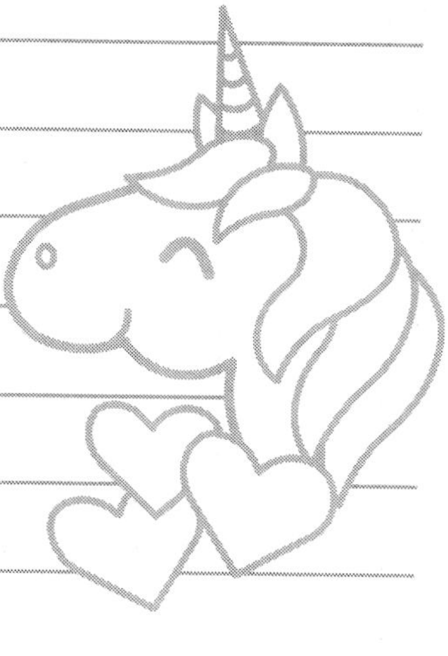

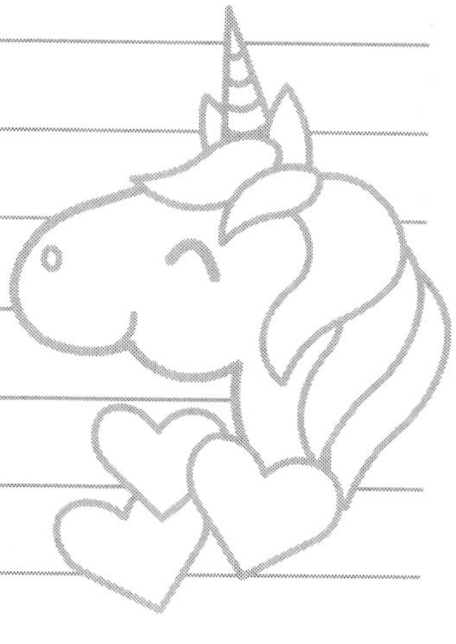

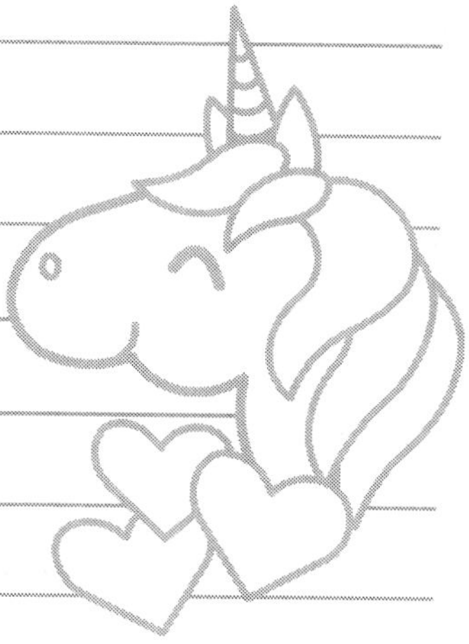

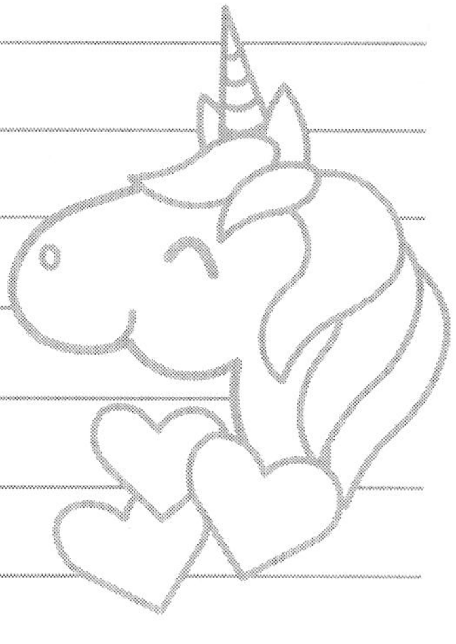

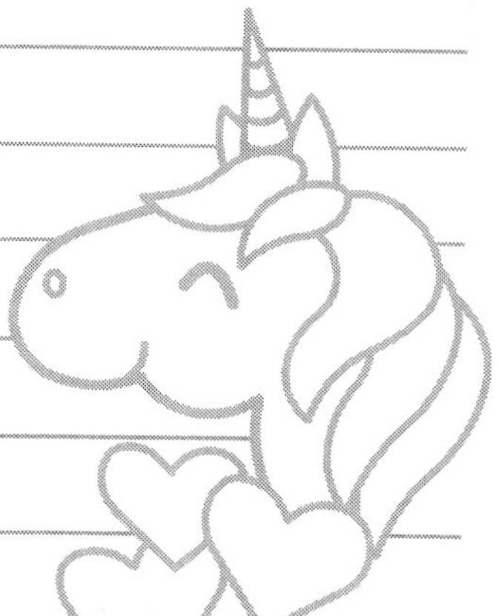

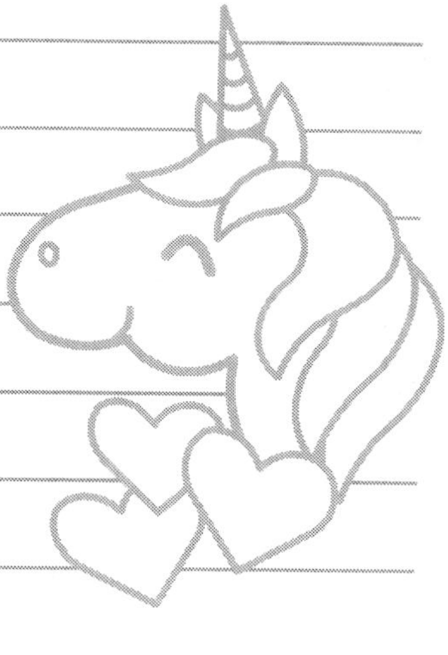

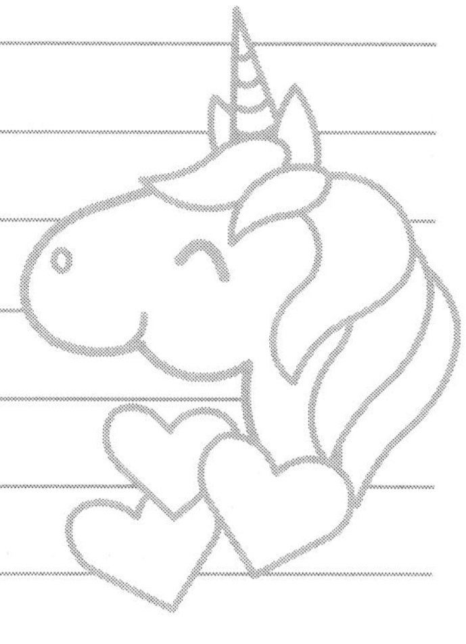

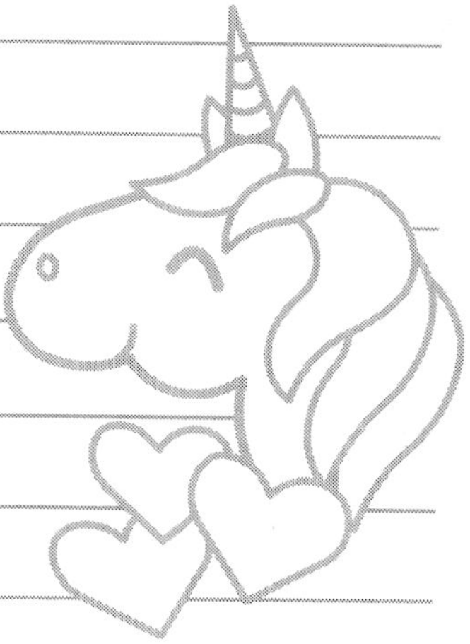

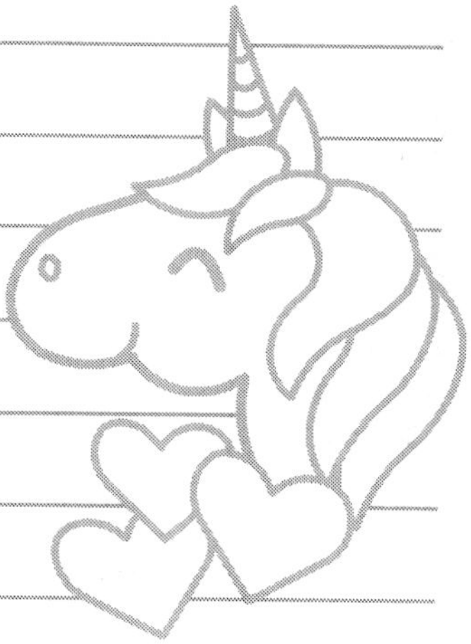

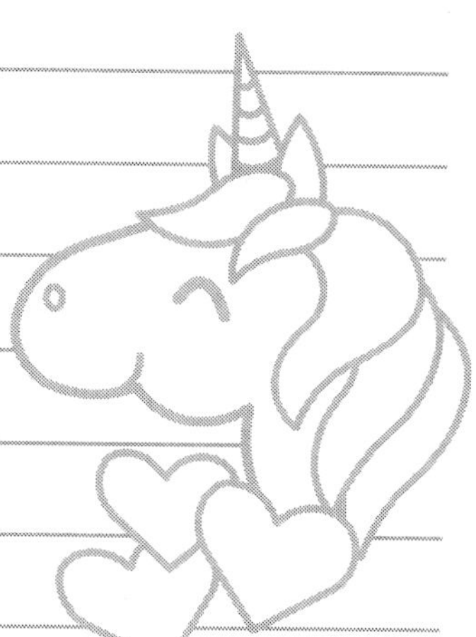

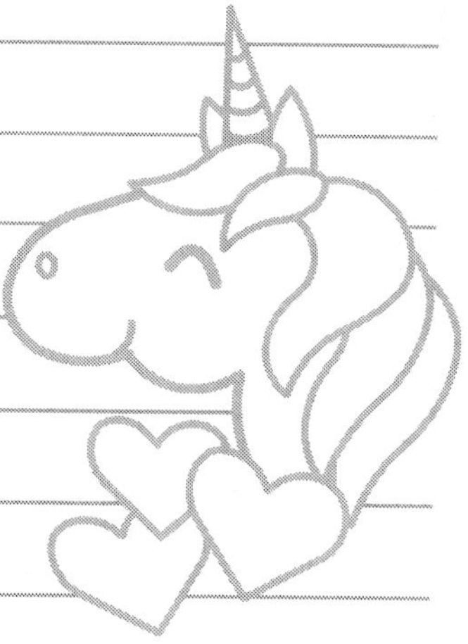

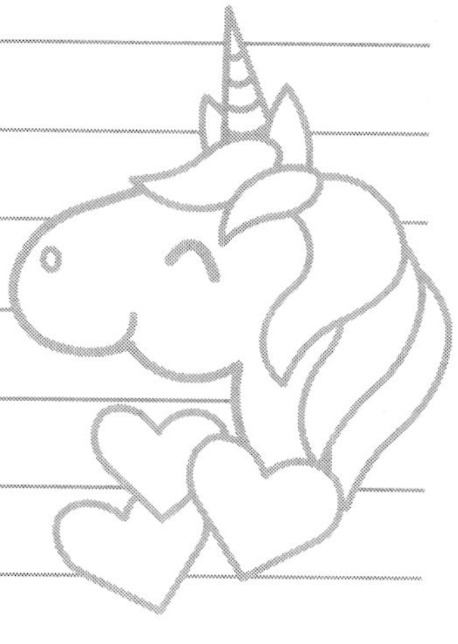

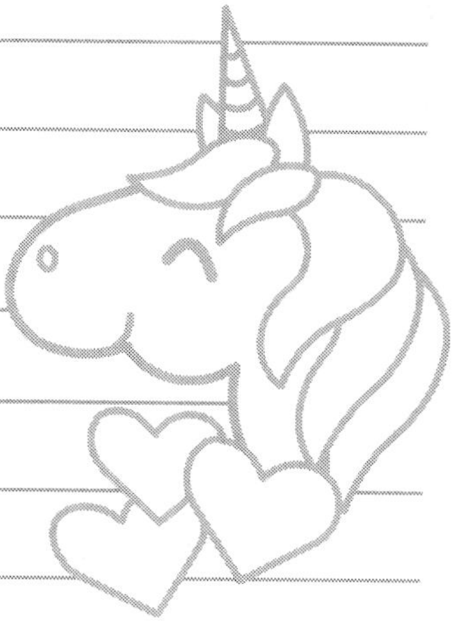

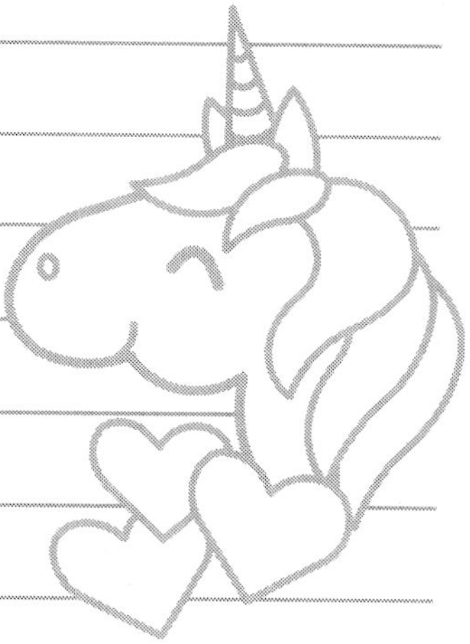

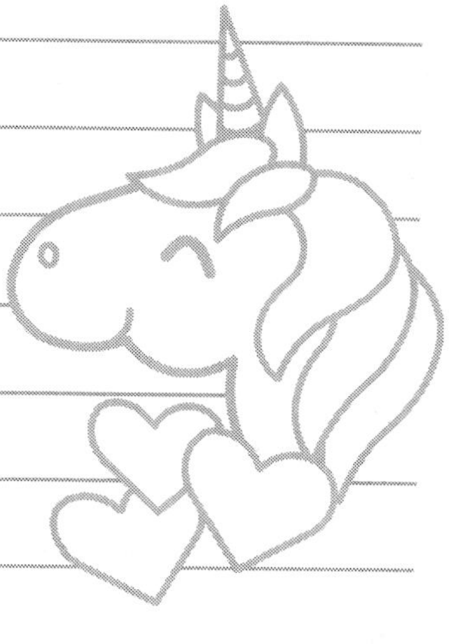

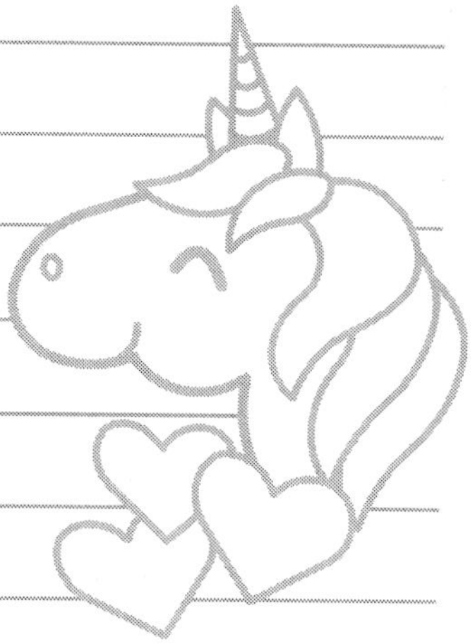

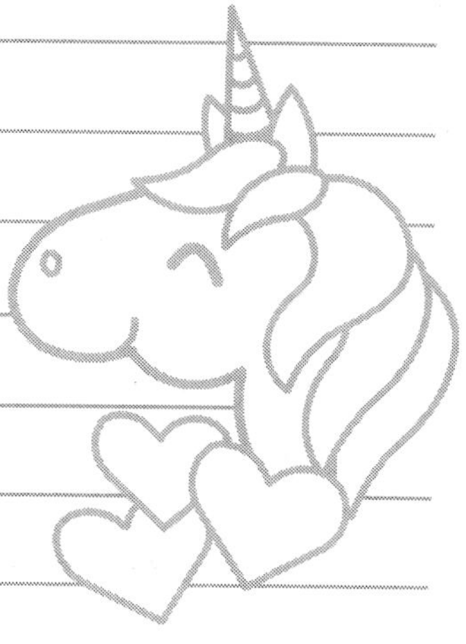

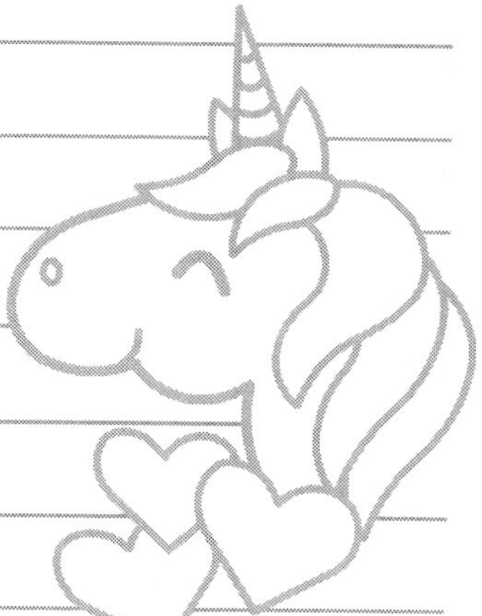

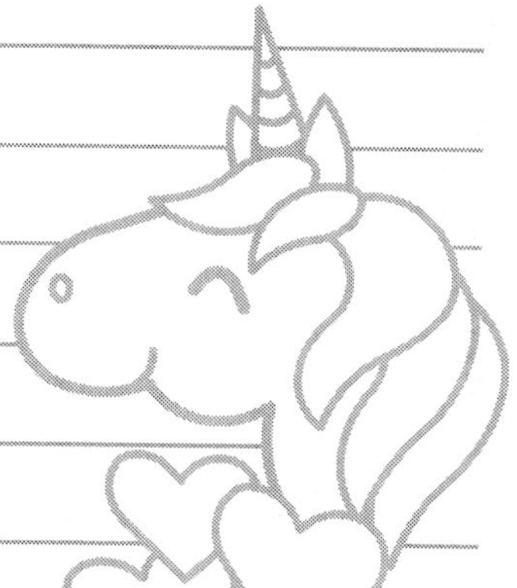

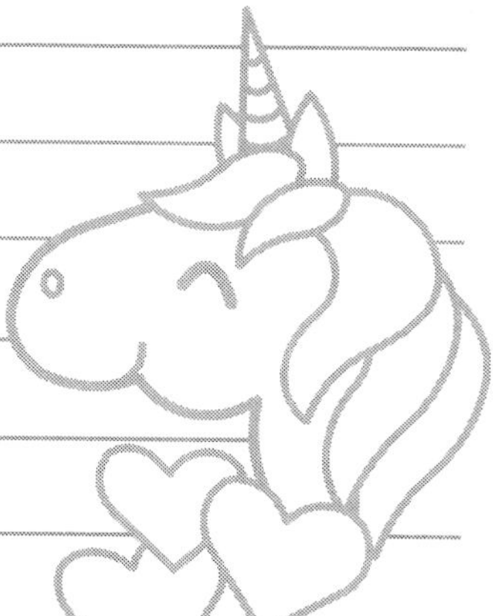

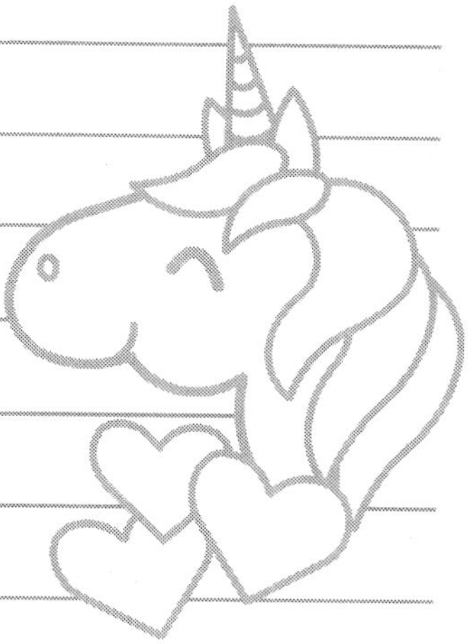

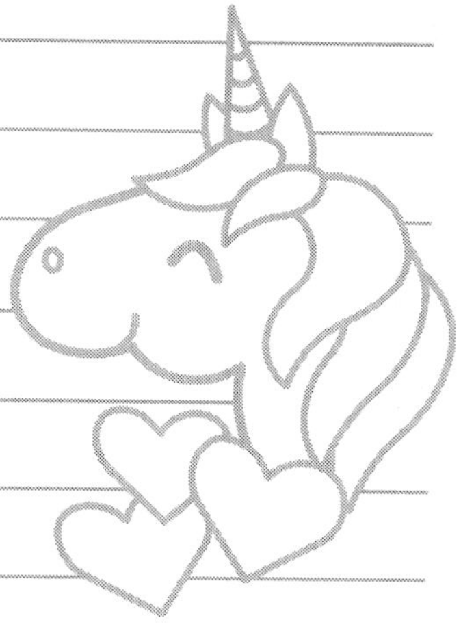

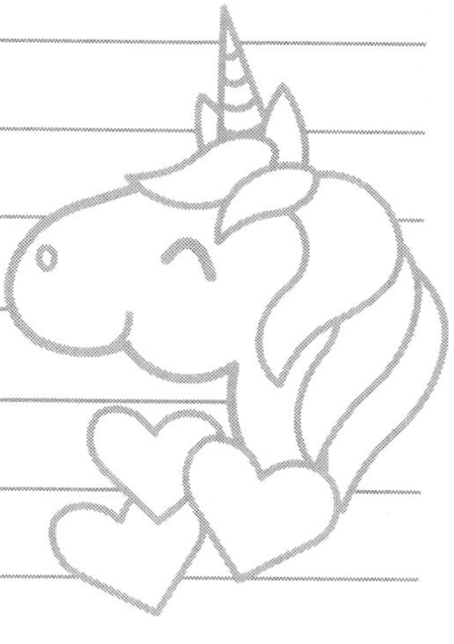

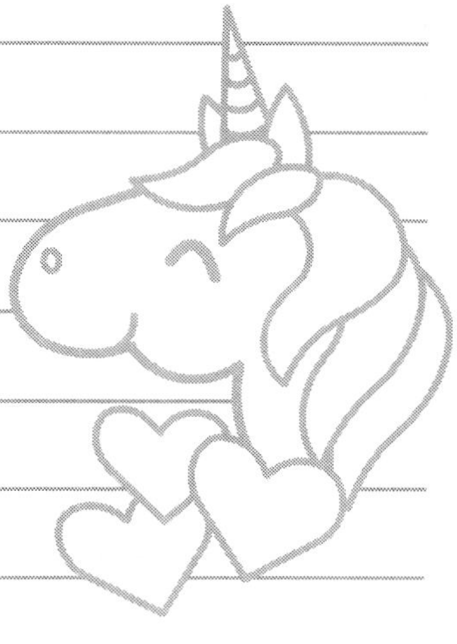

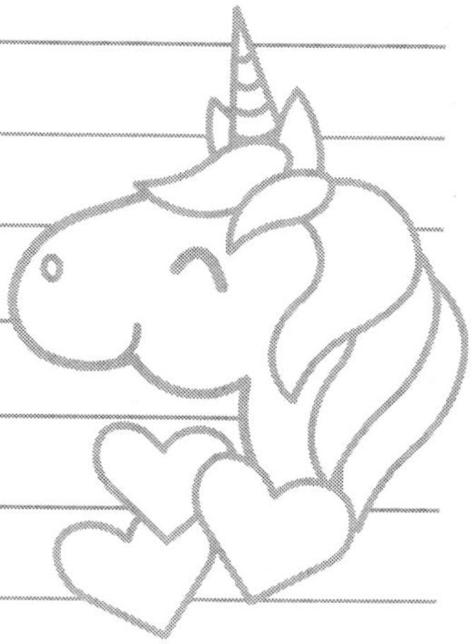

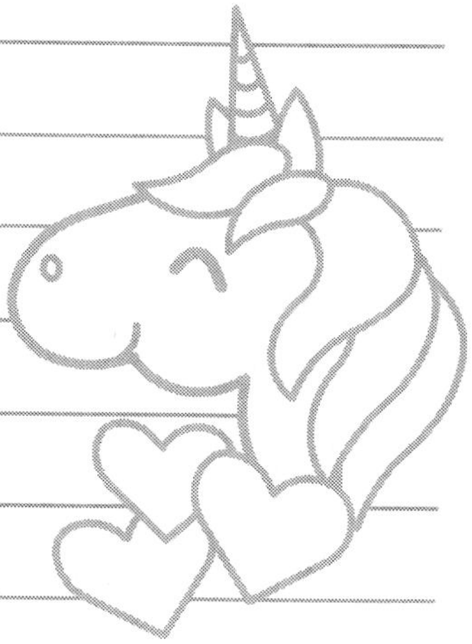

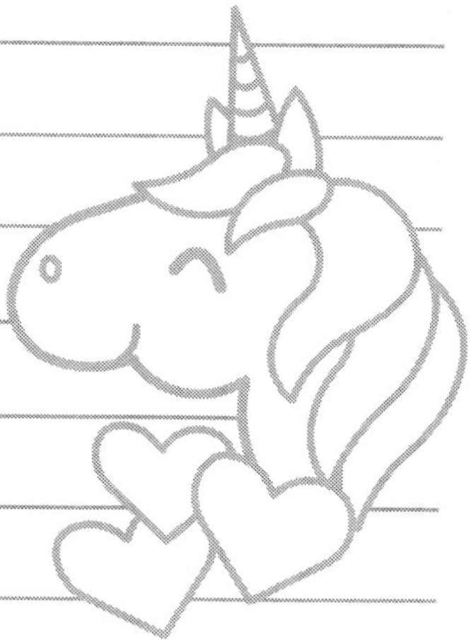

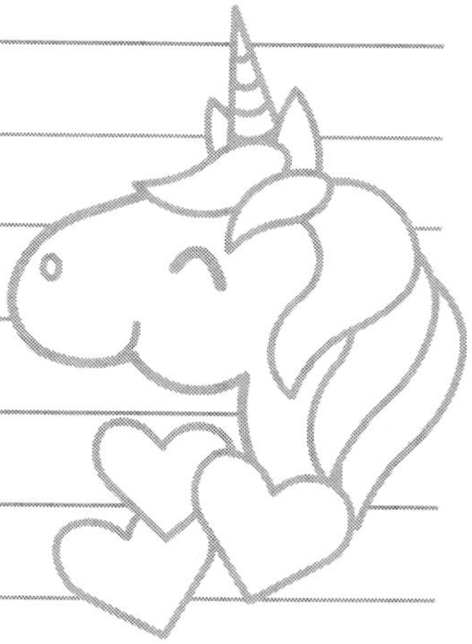

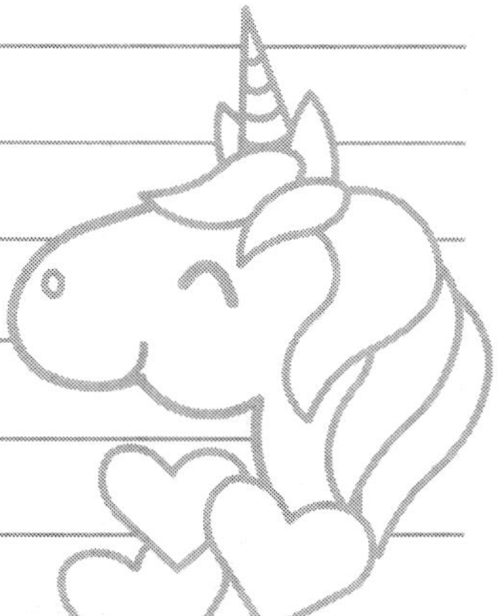

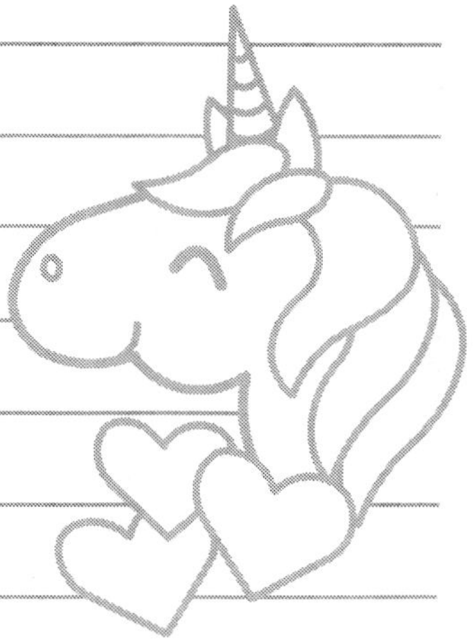

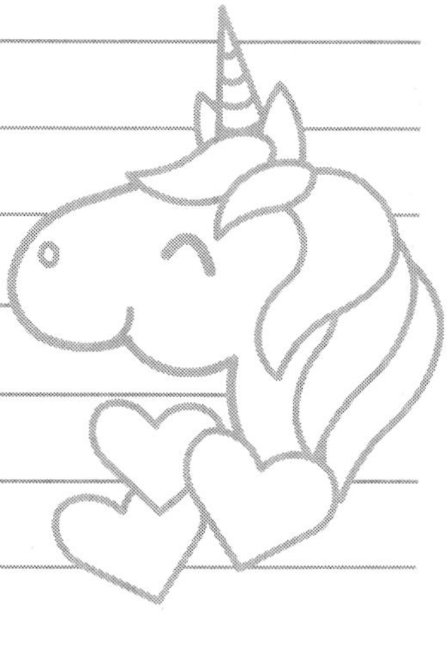

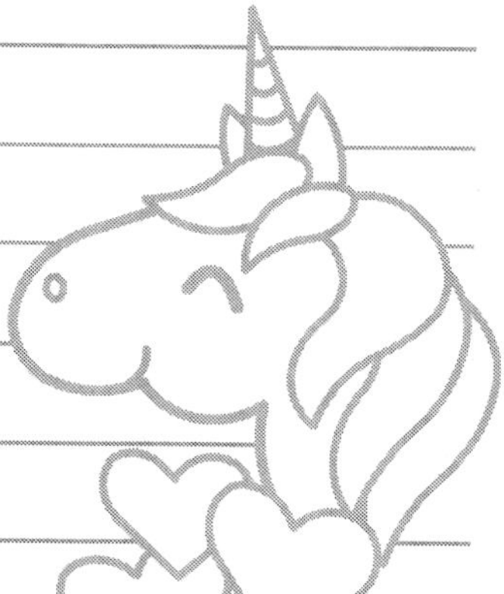

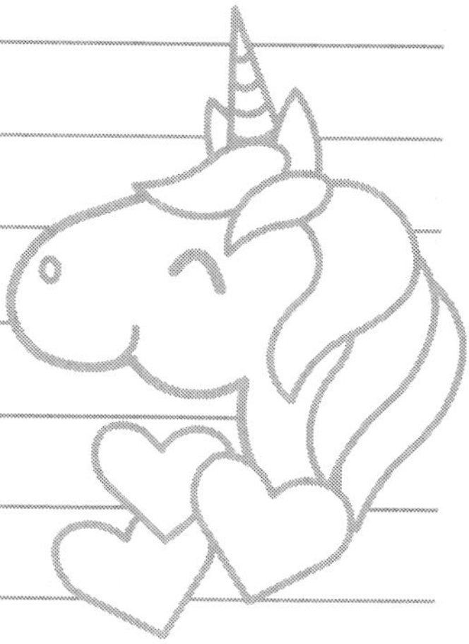

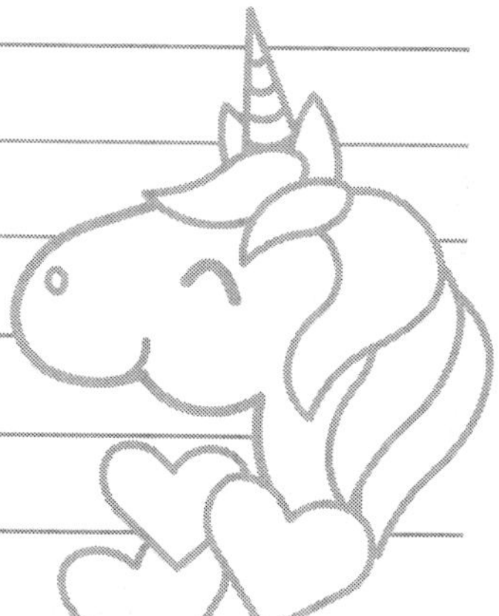

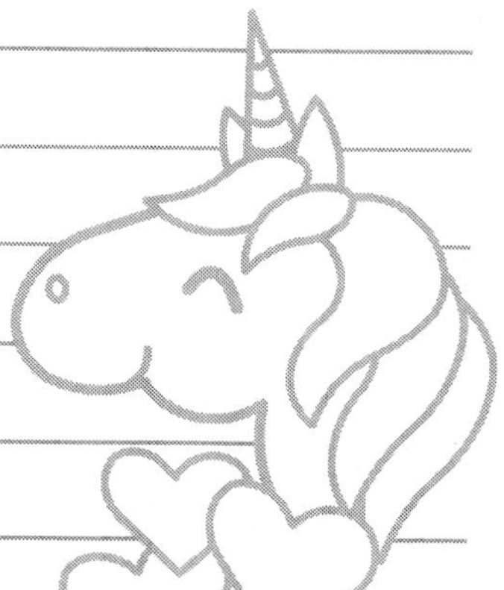

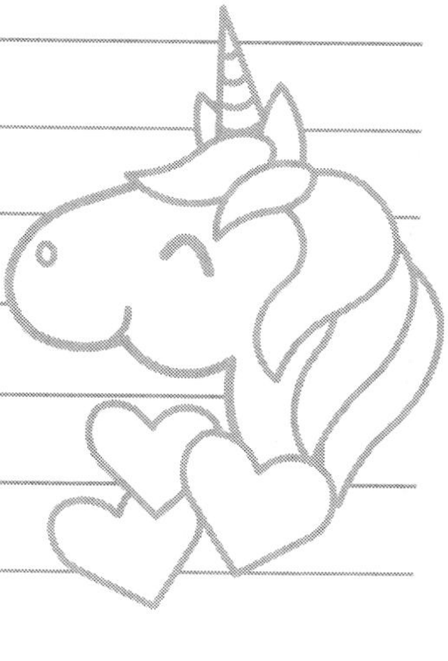

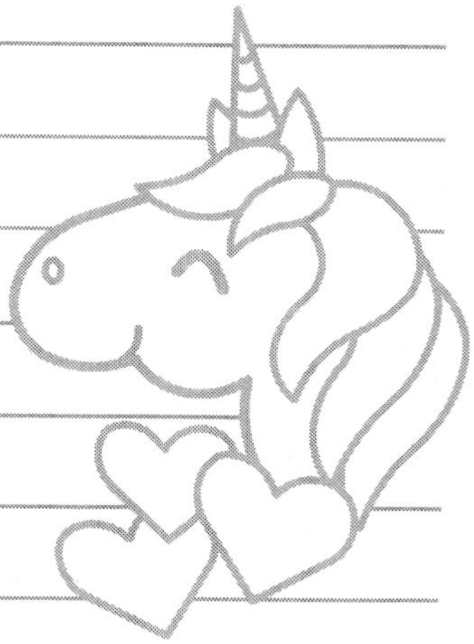

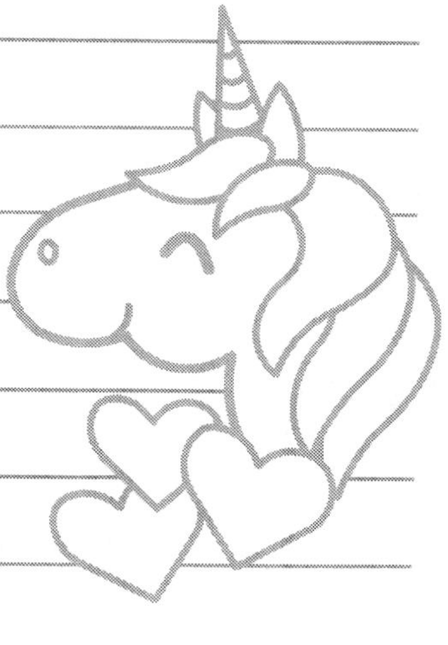

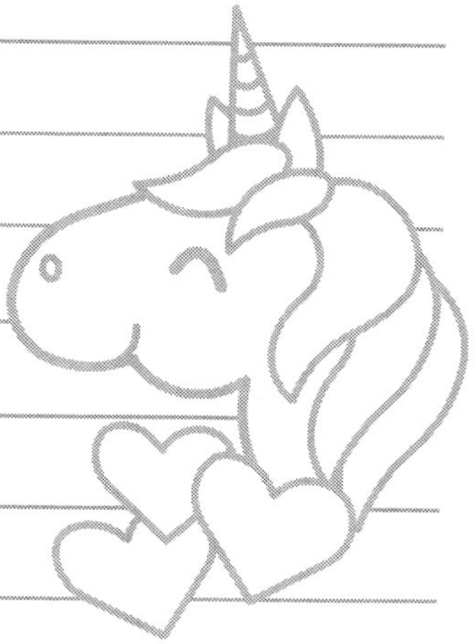

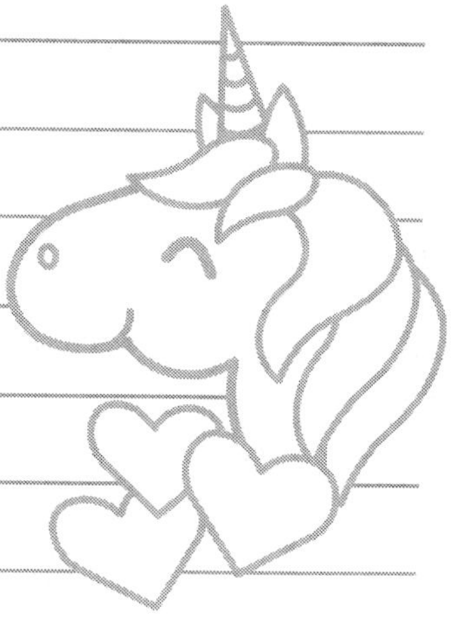

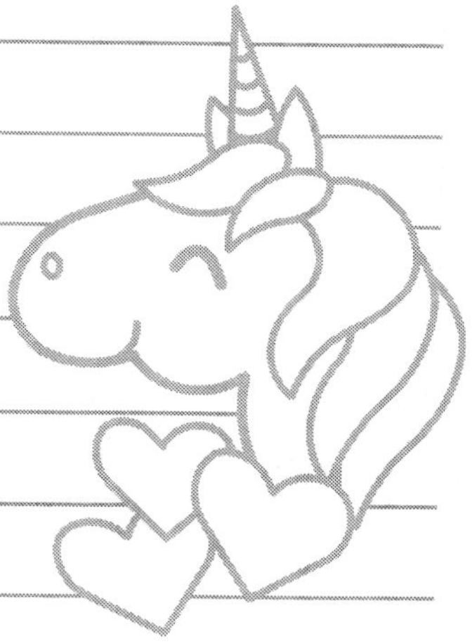

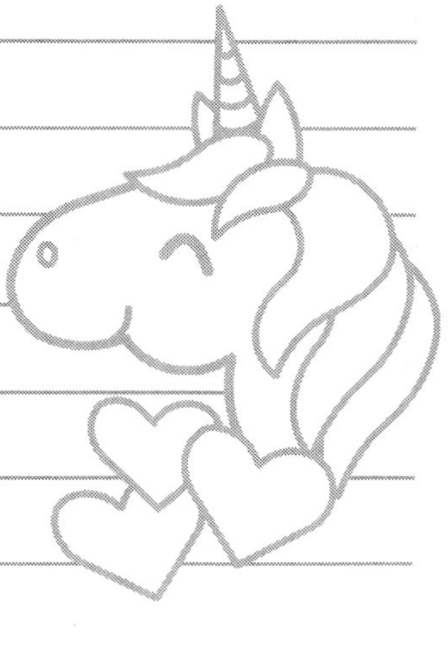

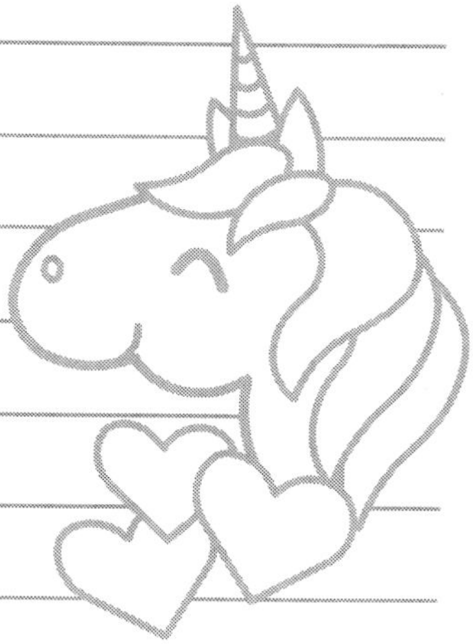

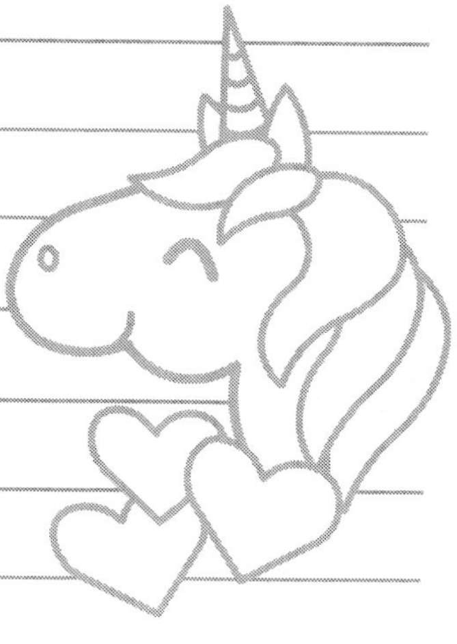

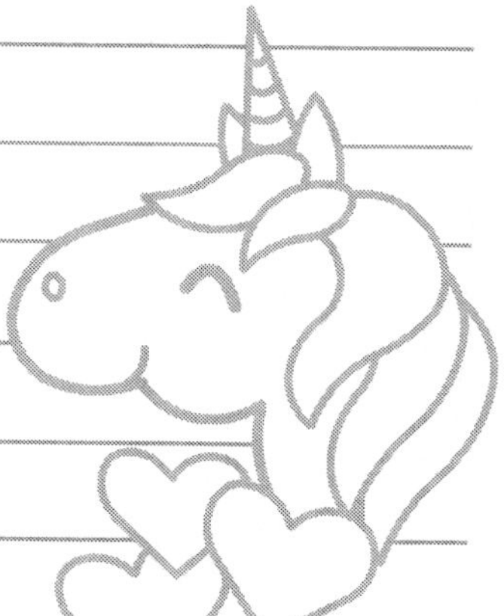

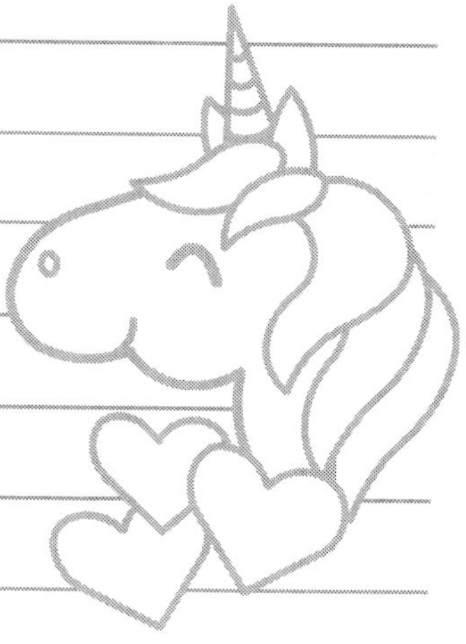

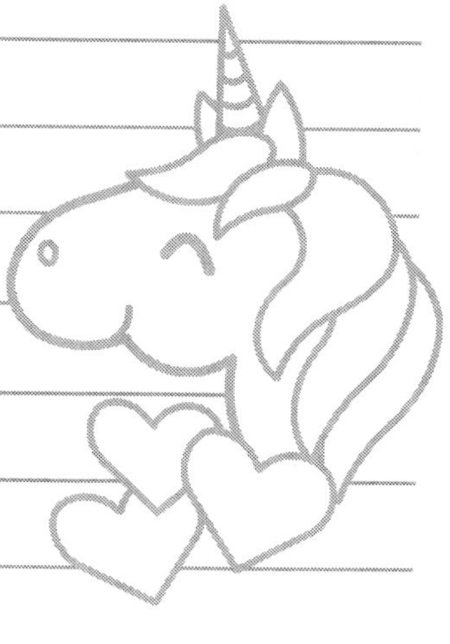

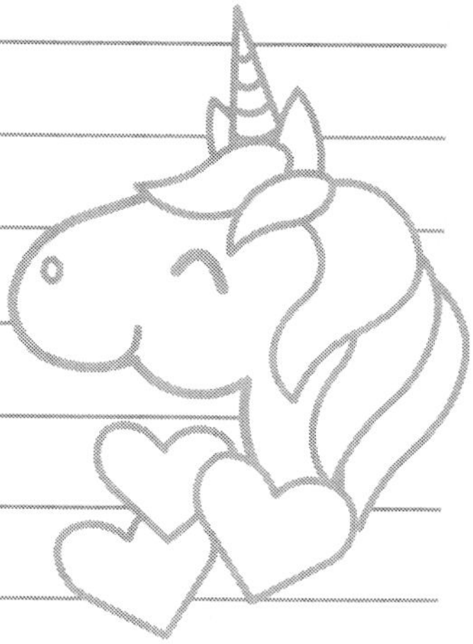

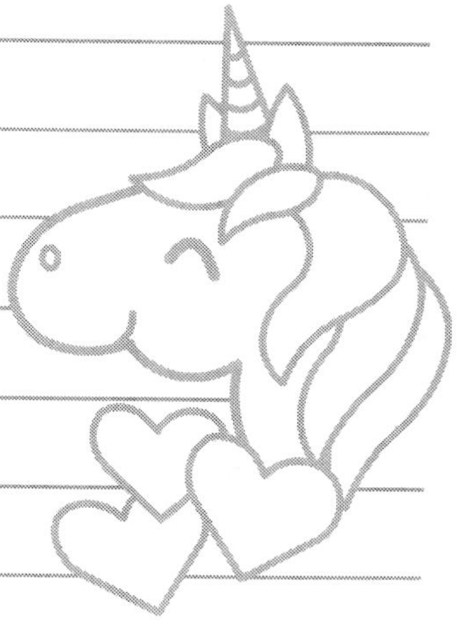

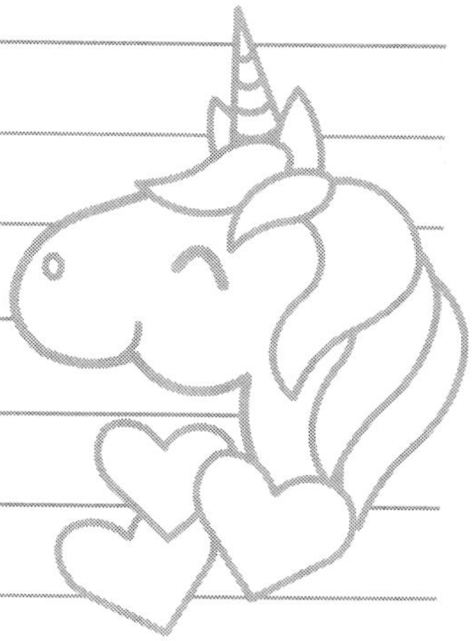

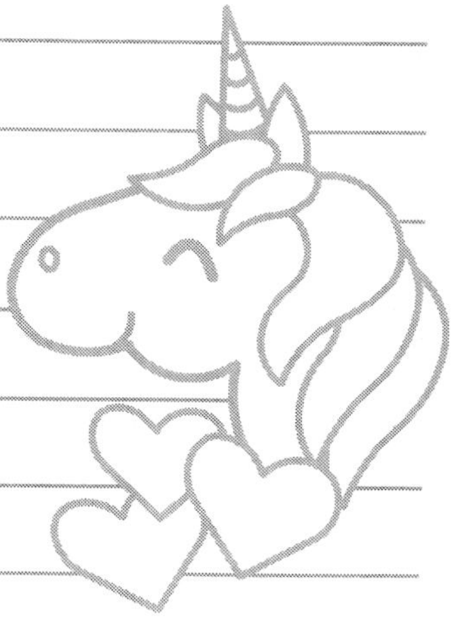

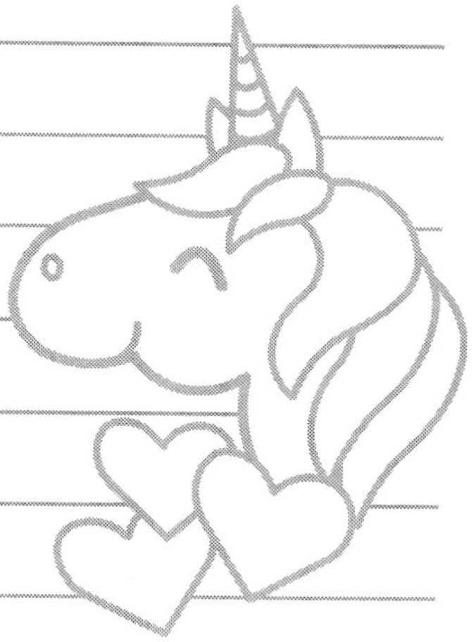

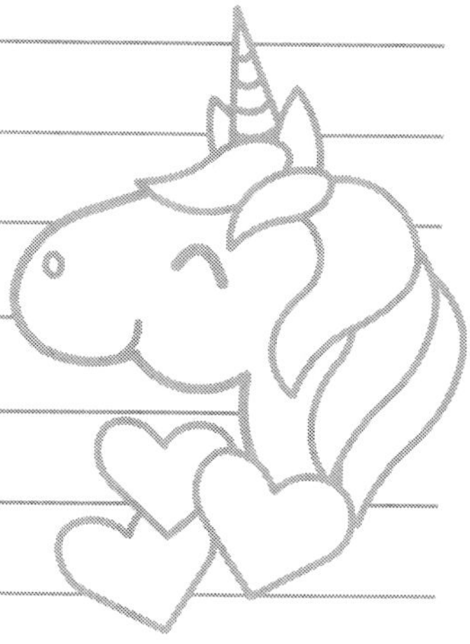

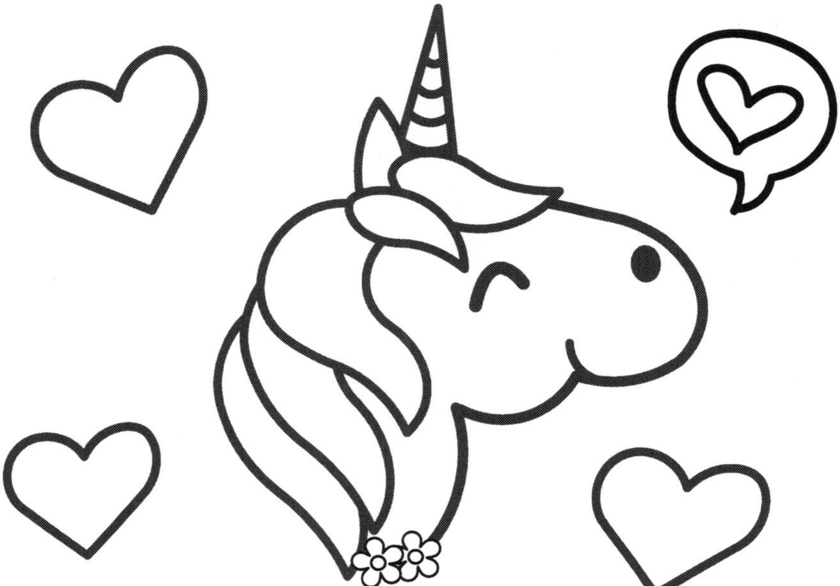

43378881R00068

Made in the USA
Middletown, DE
23 April 2019